READERS

BEGINNING TO READ ALONE **2**

Let's Go Riding!

Written by Annabel Blackledge

Today is a big day for Olivia.
She is going to have
her first riding lesson.

Olivia has everything she
needs for her lesson.
She has a smart t-shirt,
a long-sleeved top and
special riding trousers
called jodhpurs (JOD-purs).
She will need to wear
a riding hat, a body protector,
gloves and riding boots.

Safety first
Riding hats and
body protectors
are made of tough
material. They will
protect your head
and body if you fall
off a pony or horse.

When Olivia arrives
at the riding stables,
she meets three other children.
They are called Alexandra,
Holly and Sammy.
They are waiting for
their first lesson, too.
Everyone is very excited
about learning to ride.

The children meet
their riding teacher.
Her name is Linda.
She tells them the names
of the ponies they will ride.

Linda shows the children
the large, grassy fields
and cosy stables
where the ponies live.

Then Linda shows the children
where they will have their lessons.
The sand is comfortable
for the ponies to walk on.
Olivia sees a girl on a pony.
She is learning how to jump.
"When I'm older
I would like to do that,"
she says to Sammy.

Olivia's pony is called Honey.
Honey's coat is golden and
her mane and tail are white.

Mane

Horse shoes
Ponies wear
metal shoes
on their
hooves to
protect them.

Honey is a calm pony, which is good when you are first learning to ride.

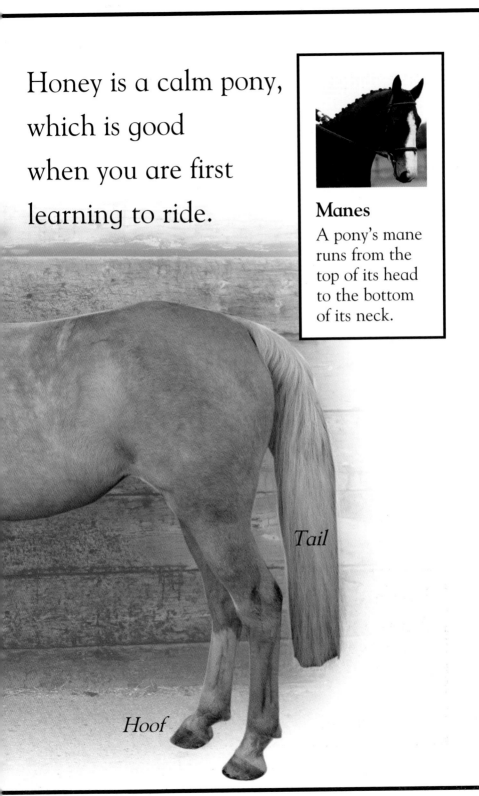

Manes

A pony's mane runs from the top of its head to the bottom of its neck.

Tail

Hoof

Alexandra's pony is called Mattie.
She is chestnut coloured
with a white mark on her face.
"She's so big!" says Alexandra.

Holly's pony
is called Woody.
He has beautiful
brown and white
patches and
a very soft coat.

Sammy will ride
a grey pony
called Bertie.
"Hold on tight,
Sammy!"
says Olivia.
Bertie looks
very strong!

The ponies need to be brushed every day to keep their coats glossy. Linda shows Olivia how to brush Honey's coat, mane and tail.

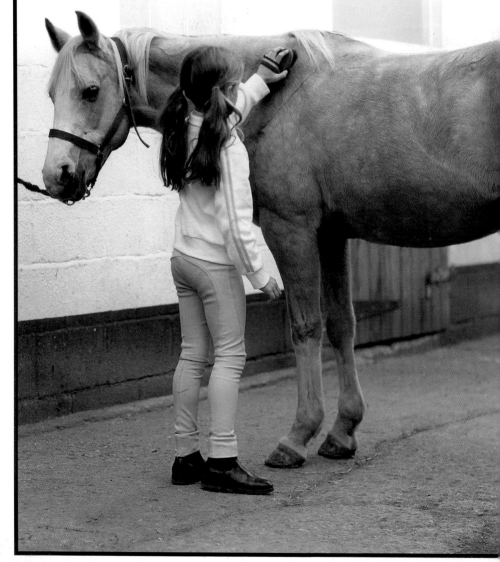

"When you brush a pony
it's called grooming,"
Linda tells the children.

Olivia grooms Honey.
"Honey is very dirty,"
Olivia says.
"It looks like
she has been rolling
in the mud."
Honey is very relaxed
when she is groomed.

Grooming kit
A grooming kit has
all the brushes and
other equipment
that are needed
to groom a pony.

"Well done, Olivia," says Linda.
"Honey looks really smart.
Now it's time to get ready."

"First of all, we need to put
a saddle on Honey so that
you can ride her,"
explains Linda.

Saddle
A saddle is a leather
seat that makes
riding comfortable
and safe for the pony
and the rider.
A cloth is put on
before the saddle.

Olivia practises putting on
the saddle by herself.
She places the saddle
gently on Honey's back.
Then she fastens the straps.

Olivia's next job
is to put on Honey's bridle.

Bridle

A bridle helps a rider
to control a pony.
It is made up of
leather straps
attached to a metal
bar called a bit.
The bit fits inside
the pony's mouth.

Olivia knows that she must be
careful and gentle with Honey.
Olivia holds the bridle
like Linda has shown her.
Then she puts the bit
into Honey's mouth and
pulls the bridle over Honey's ears.

At last, it is time
for Olivia to ride Honey.
Linda shows Olivia how to get on.
"Getting on a pony
is called mounting," Linda says.

Olivia feels nervous.
"Honey is too big,"
she says.
"I don't think
I can climb
up there."

"Yes you can,"
says Linda.

So Olivia has a try.
She puts her left foot
in the foot support
called a stirrup,
and holds on
to the saddle.

She springs up and
swings her right leg
over the saddle.
"Hooray, I did it!"
she says.

Olivia sits up straight
in the saddle and
tries to relax.

The children line up
on their ponies.
"Let's do some warm-up exercises,"
says Linda.
"They will help you learn
to trust your pony."

First the children reach back
and touch their pony's tail.

Then they reach down
and touch their toes.

Finally, they reach forwards
and touch their pony's head.
"Stretch, Sammy!" calls Olivia.
"I'm trying!" Sammy laughs.

Olivia loves riding Honey.
The children ride their ponies
round and round.
Olivia feels like a real rider, now.

Wild horses
Horses in the wild
live in groups
called herds.
They eat, sleep
and move about
all together.

Alexandra and Mattie
lead the way.
The children enjoy playing
follow-my-leader.

The lesson is nearly over.
Linda asks the children
to line up on their ponies
so she can talk to them.
"I hope you have enjoyed
your first riding lesson," she says.

"I liked sitting up high on Honey,"
says Olivia.
"I liked stroking
Woody's soft mane," says Holly.
"I liked everything!"
says Sammy.

"Now it's time to get off
your pony," says Linda.
"This is called dismounting."
Linda shows the children
the right way to dismount.

Olivia takes her feet
out of the stirrups.
Then she swings her leg over and
slides down to the ground.

Sammy does not want
to leave Bertie.
"Don't worry, Sammy,"
says Linda kindly.
"You can ride Bertie
again next week."

Olivia says goodbye to Honey.

She strokes her soft nose.

"Good girl, Honey," she says.

"I can't wait to ride you again.

I want to learn how to trot,

gallop and jump!"

Fascinating facts

Horses and ponies are measured in hands. One hand is the same as 10 centimetres (4 inches). Ponies are smaller than horses.

You can tell how horses and ponies are feeling by looking at their ears. If their ears are sticking up straight and facing forwards, it means that they are happy.

Horses and ponies belong to the same animal family as zebras. Their bodies are the same shape and they both have hooves and a mane. Wild zebras live in herds, like wild horses do.

Horses and ponies spend most of the time standing, but sometimes they roll around on the grass or in the mud.